I'm still
A HOT BABE

~~~~~~~~~~~~~~~~~~~~

BUT NOW IT COMES
in
Flashes

I'm still A HOT BABE

BUT NOW IT COMES *in* *Flashes*

CAROL LYNN PEARSON

GIBBS SMITH
TO ENRICH AND INSPIRE HUMANKIND

First Edition
20 19 18 17 16   20 19 18 17 16 15 14 13 12 11 10 9 8 7 6 5 4

Published by
Gibbs Smith
P.O. Box 667
Layton, Utah 84041

1.800.835.4993 orders
www.gibbs-smith.com

Cover design by Black Eye Design
Designed by Melissa Dymock
Printed and bound in China
Gibbs Smith books are printed on either recycled, 100% post-consumer
waste, FSC-certified papers or on paper produced from sustainable PEFC-
certified forest/controlled wood source. Learn more at www.pefc.org.

Library of Congress Cataloging-in-Publication Data
Pearson, Carol Lynn.
  I'm still a hot babe, but now it comes in flashes / Carol Lynn Pearson. — 1st ed.
      p. cm.
  ISBN 978-1-4236-2023-5
 1. Women—Humor. I. Title.
  PN6231.W6P43 2011
  818'.5402—dc22
                              2010037776

Contents

Chapter 1

Go with the Flow

Sign over a gynecologist's office:

"Dr. Jones, at your cervix."

Did you hear about the
cross-eyed seamstress?

She couldn't mend straight.

Favorite Euphemisms For Menstrual Period:

Miss Scarlett's Come Home to Tara

Saddling Old Rusty

Auntie Flo's in Town

Playing Banjo in Sgt. Zygote's Ragtime Band

Arts and Crafts Week at Panty Camp

Rebooting the Ovarian Operating System

Game Day for the Crimson Tide

The Red Coats are coming!

BUT NOW IT COMES IN FLASHES

*T*hree boys are walking down Main Street trying to decide what to do for entertainment with their combined twenty dollars. Should they go to a movie? Buy a football? Play in the arcade?

"Wait a sec!" says one of the boys as he runs into the drug store. A few minutes later he comes out with a package of tampons. "You idiot!" his friends shout. "We wanted to have some fun. What are we going to do with those?"

"Look what it says right here on the box," the boy replies. " 'With these you can go horseback riding, you can go swimming . . .'"

There will be no more
menstruation jokes.

Period!

PMS? Who, me?

No, I don't have PMS. Why do you ask?

AND WHO THE HELL SAID YOU

COULD TALK TO ME ANYHOW?

A study conducted by UCLA's Department of Psychiatry has revealed that the kind of face a woman finds attractive on a man can differ depending on where she is in her menstrual cycle. For example: If she is ovulating, she is attracted to men with rugged and masculine features. However, if she is menstruating or menopausal, she tends to prefer a man with scissors lodged in his temple and a bat jammed up his butt while he is on fire.

What does PMS stand for?

Puffy Mid Section

Pissy Mood Syndrome

Pardon My Sobbing

Perpetual Munching Spree

Pass My Shotgun

Pack My Stuff

Pushing My Sanity

Potential Murder Suspect

Juliet with PMS:

"Romeo, Romeo, where the hell are ya, Romeo???"

My gynecologist laughed
when I told him how bitchy
I get during my period.

So I shot him.

A preacher was telling his congregation that anything they could think of, old or new, was discussed somewhere in the Bible and that the entirety of the human experience could be found there.

After the service, he was approached by a woman who said, "Preacher, I don't believe the Bible mentions PMS."

The preacher replied that he was sure it must be there somewhere and that he would look for it.

The following week after the service, the preacher called the woman aside and showed her a passage that read, "And Mary rode Joseph's ass all the way to Bethlehem."

One thing that I have never fully understood about PMS is how women have it at a certain time of the month, **WHILE MEN SEEM TO HAVE IT ALL MONTH LONG.**

This handy guide for dealing with a woman who has PMS should be in the wallet of every husband, boyfriend or significant other!

DANGEROUS: What's for dinner?

SAFER: Can I help you with dinner?

SAFEST: Where would you like to go for dinner?

ULTRA SAFE: Here, have some wine.

DANGEROUS: Are you wearing that?

SAFER: Hey, you sure look good in brown!

SAFEST: WOW! Look at you!

ULTRA SAFE: Here, have some wine.

DANGEROUS: What are you so worked up about?

SAFER: Could we be overreacting?

SAFEST: Here's my paycheck.

ULTRA SAFE: Here, have some wine.

DANGEROUS: Should you be eating that?

SAFER: You know, there are a lot of apples left.

SAFEST: Can I get you a piece of chocolate with that?

ULTRA SAFE: Here, have some wine.

DANGEROUS: What did you DO all day?

SAFER: I hope you didn't overdo it today.

SAFEST: I've always loved you in that robe!

ULTRA SAFE: Here, have some wine.

If women ran the world we wouldn't have wars, just intense negotiations every twenty-eight days.

—*Robin Williams*

My husband, being unhappy with my mood swings, bought me a mood ring the other day so he would be able to monitor my moods. We've discovered that when I'm in a good mood, it turns green and when I'm in a bad mood, it leaves a big red mark on his forehead.

Next time he'd better get me a diamond!

Women complain about premenstrual syndrome, but I think of it as the only time of the month I can be myself.

—Roseanne

Chapter 2

Thanks for the Mammaries!

Q: Why is it called "The Wonder Bra"?

A: When she takes it off, you wonder where her boobs went.

Q: Why did the moron girl swimmer lose the Olympics?

A: Because the event was for the breast stroke and all the other girls used their arms!

"A recent study found that 35% of men have been injured while undoing a woman's bra— strained tendons, scratches, and other similar injuries. Actually, I got injured today while trying to undo a woman's bra. *She was in front of me in the checkout line, and she turned and hit me with a can of peas.*"

A lot of guys think the larger a woman's breasts are, the less intelligent she is. I don't think it works like that. I think it's the opposite. I think the larger a woman's breasts are, the less intelligent men become.

—Anita Wise

Have you ever wondered why A, B, C, D, DD, E, F and G are the letters used to define bra sizes?

A—Almost boobs

B—Barely there

C—Can't complain

D—Damn!

DD—Double damn!

E—Enormous!

F—Fake

G—Get a reduction!

What religion is your bra?

A man walked into the ladies department of a Macy's and shyly walked up to the woman behind the counter and said, "I'd like to buy a bra for my wife."

"What type of bra?" asked the clerk.

"Type?" inquired the man, "There's more than one type?"

"Look around," said the saleslady, as she showed a sea of bras in every shape, size, color and material imaginable. "Actually, even with all of this variety, there are really only four types of bras to choose from."

Relieved, the man asked about the types.

The saleslady replied, "There are the Catholic, the Salvation Army, the Presbyterian, and the Baptist types. Which one would you prefer?"

Now totally befuddled, the man asked about the differences between them.

The saleslady responded, "It is all really quite simple . . .

The Catholic type supports the masses—

The Salvation Army type lifts the fallen—

The Presbyterian type keeps them staunch and upright—and

The Baptist type makes mountains out of mole hills."

A girl with a lisp goes to the doctor to have her cold treated. The doctor lifts up her top to listen to her chest and says, "Nice big breaths."

The girl replies, "Yeth, and I'm only fourteen."

I was the first woman to burn my bra—it took the fire department four days to put it out.

—*Dolly Parton*

The success of the "Wonder Bra" for under-endowed women has encouraged the designers to come out with a new bra for over-endowed women. It's called the "Sheep Dog Bra."

IT ROUNDS 'EM UP AND POINTS 'EM IN THE RIGHT DIRECTION.

Whoever thought up the word "mammogram"? Every time I hear it, I think I'm supposed to put my breast in an envelope and send it to someone.

—Jan King

**There are three reasons
for breastfeeding:**

The milk is always at the
right temperature

It comes in attractive containers

The cat can't get it

—*Irena Chalmers*

A woman with a baby comes into the doctor's office. She is told to go into a room and wait for the doctor. After arriving, the doctor examines the baby and asks the woman, "Is he breastfed or on the bottle?"

"Breastfed," she replies.

"Well, strip down to your waist," the doctor orders.

She does.

He presses, kneads, pinches both breasts for a while in a detailed examination. Then, motioning for her to get dressed, the doctor says, "No wonder this baby is hungry. You don't have any milk."

"Naturally," she says, "I'm his aunt. But I'm glad I came."

Q: What's a lap dance?

A: Twin babies simultaneously breastfeeding.

Q: When is your child too old to continue breastfeeding?

A: When he invites his friends over for dinner.

Ladies, it is amazing how you do that, with a beverage coming out of your nipple, did you know that? Guys, we can't do it. Because if we could, we'd spend the whole time squirting each other.

—*Dave Attell*

My mother, she never breastfed me.
She told me she liked me as a friend.

–*Rodney Dangerfield*

Many women are afraid of their first mammogram, but there is no need to worry. By taking a few minutes each day for a week preceding the exam and doing the following practice exercises, you will be totally prepared, and best of all, you can do these simple practice exercises right in your home.

Exercise 1:

Open your refrigerator and insert one breast between the door and the main box. Have one of your strongest friends slam the door shut as hard as possible and lean on the door for good measure. Hold that position for five seconds. Repeat once or twice for good measure.

Exercise 2:

Visit your garage at 3 a.m. when the temperature of the
cement floor is just perfect. Take off all your clothes and
lie comfortably on the floor with one breast wedged under
the rear tire of the car. Ask a friend to slowly back the car
up until your breast is sufficiently flattened and chilled. Turn
over and repeat for the other breast.

Exercise 3:

Freeze two metal bookends overnight. Strip to the waist. Invite a stranger into the room to press the bookends against one of your breasts. Smash the bookends together as hard as you can. Set an appointment with the stranger to meet next year and do it again.

Chapter 3

The Sex Factor

Men reach their sexual peak at eighteen. Women reach theirs at thirty-five. Do you get the feeling that God is playing a practical joke?

—Rita Rudner

Every girl should use what
Mother Nature gave her before
Father Time takes it away.

—*Laurence J. Peter*

There are three possible parts to a date, of which at least two must be offered: entertainment, food, and affection. It is customary to begin a series of dates with a great deal of entertainment, a moderate amount of food, and the merest suggestion of affection. As the amount of affection increases, the entertainment can be reduced proportionately. When the affection is the entertainment, we no longer call it dating. Under no circumstances can the food be omitted.

—Miss Manners' Guide to
Excruciatingly Correct Behaviour

Men wake up aroused in the morning.
We can't help it. We just wake up and
we want you. And the women are
thinking, "How can he want me the way
I look in the morning?" It's because
we can't see you. We have no blood
anywhere near our optic nerve.

—Andy Rooney

I think I could fall MADLY
in bed WITH YOU.

Nymphomaniac: a woman as obsessed with sex as an average man.

—Mignon McLaughlin, *The Neurotic's Notebook*

It is not economical to go to
bed early to save the candles
if the result is twins.

–Chinese Proverb

Don't have sex, man. It leads to kissing and pretty soon you have to start talking to them.

—Steve Martin

Sex is a bad thing because
it rumples the clothes.

–Jacqueline Kennedy Onassis

If someone had told me years ago that sharing a sense of humor was so vital to partnerships, I could have avoided a lot of sex.

—Kate Beckinsale

It doesn't matter what you do in the bedroom as long as you don't do it in the street and frighten the horses.

—Mrs. Patrick Campbell

Women might be able to fake orgasms.

But men are able to fake a whole relationship.

—Sharon Stone

Q: What's the difference between a g-spot and a golf ball?

A: A man will spend twenty minutes looking for a golf ball.

Sex is the most fun
you can have without laughing.

—Woody Allen

Chapter 4

It's Going to Be a
Long Nine Months

Love is all fun and games
until someone loses an
eye or gets pregnant.

–Jim Cole

Never go to your high school reunion
pregnant or they will think that is
all you have done since you graduated.

—*Erma Bombeck*

Q: What do you call a pregnancy that begins while using birth control?

A: A misconception.

Q: What's the difference between a pregnant woman and a lightbulb?

A: You can unscrew a lightbulb.

By far the most common craving of pregnant women is NOT TO BE PREGNANT.

—*Phyllis Diller*

Life is tough enough
without having someone
kick you from the inside.

–Rita Rudner

Definitions for the Mother-To-Be

PREGNANT PAUSE: The amount of time it takes for a nine-month pregnant woman to get out of a chair.

PRENATAL: When your life was still your own.

AMNESIA: Condition that enables a woman who has gone through labor to make love again.

You should never say anything to a woman that even remotely suggests that you think she's pregnant unless you can see an actual baby emerging from her at that moment.

—Dave Barry

One terrific thing that happened during pregnancy was the way my breasts developed. It was probably the only time in my life that I could look into a mirror and ask, "Mirror, Mirror, on the wall, who is the fairest of them all?" and not have the mirror answer, "You are, Sir."

—*Joan Rivers*

*B*renda, pregnant with her first child, was paying a visit to her obstetrician's office. When the exam was over, she shyly began, "My husband wants me to ask you if it's still okay . . ."

"I know, I know," the doctor said, placing a reassuring hand on her shoulder, "I get asked that all the time. Sex is fine until late in the pregnancy."

"No, that's not it at all," Brenda confessed. "He wants to know if I can still mow the lawn."

Q: Am I more likely to get pregnant if my husband wears boxers rather than briefs?

A: Yes, but you're even more likely if he wears nothing at all.

Q: How will I know if my vomiting is morning sickness or the flu?

A: If it's the flu, you'll get better.

Q: What position should I expect my baby to be in during the last month of pregnancy?

A: Face down, pressing firmly on your bladder.

Q: What happens to disposable diapers
after they're thrown away?

A: They are stored in a silo in the
Midwest in the event of global
chemical warfare.

Q: What is the best cure for morning sickness?

A: Don't get up until mid-afternoon.

Q: Can a mother get pregnant while nursing?

A: Yes, but it's much easier if she removes the baby from her breast and puts him to sleep first.

Q: Should I have a baby after 35?

A: No, 35 children is enough for anybody.

Q: I'm two months pregnant now. When will my baby move?

A: With any luck, right after he finishes college.

Chapter 5

Stand and Deliver
(or Lie Down if You Must)

Somewhere on this globe, every ten seconds, there is a woman giving birth to a child. She must be found and stopped.

—Sam Levenson

Now the thing about having a baby—and I can't be the first person to have noticed this—is that thereafter you have it.

—*Jean Kerr*

When I was born I was so surprised
I didn't talk for a year and a half.

—*Gracie Allen*

~~~~~~~~~~~~~~~~~~~

Giving birth is like taking your lower
lip and forcing it over your head.

—*Carol Burnett*

Almost every pregnant woman approaches the big event with fear and trepidation. My cousin Shirley screamed and screamed when she was having her baby. And that was just conception!

— Joan Rivers

People are giving birth underwater now.
They say it's less traumatic for the
baby because it's in water. But certainly more
traumatic for the other people in the pool.

—Elayne Boosler

If men had to have babies, they would only ever have one each.

—Princess Diana

The best contraceptive is a glass of cold water—not before or after, **BUT INSTEAD OF.**

My best birth control now is just to leave the lights on.

—Joan Rivers

On a maternity room door:

"Push. Push. Push."

Chapter 6

A Night Sweat
to Remember

Mother earth is going
through some changes.

**Expect hot flushes, deforestation
and uncontrollable flooding.**

Seven Dwarfs of Menopause:

Itchy

Bitchy

Sweaty

Sleepy

Bloated

Forgetful

All Dried Up

The most important thing men need to know about menopause is that jokes about menopause can be HAZARDOUS TO THEIR HEALTH.

Q: How many women with MENOPAUSE does it take to change a light bulb?

A: One! ONLY ONE!!!! And do you know WHY? Because no one else in this house knows HOW to change a light bulb!

They don't even know that the bulb is BURNED OUT! They would sit in the dark for THREE DAYS before they figured it out.

And, once they figured it out, they wouldn't be able to find the #&%!* light bulbs despite the fact that they've been in the SAME CABINET for the past SEVENTEEN YEARS!

But if they did, by some miracle of God, actually find them, TWO DAYS LATER, the chair they dragged to stand on to change the STUPID light bulb would STILL BE IN THE SAME SPOT!! AND UNDERNEATH IT WOULD BE THE WRAPPER THE FREAKING LIGHT BULBS CAME IN!! BECAUSE NO ONE EVER PICKS UP OR CARRIES OUT THE GARBAGE! IT'S A WONDER WE HAVEN'T ALL SUFFOCATED FROM THE PILES OF GARBAGE THAT ARE A FOOT DEEP THROUGHOUT THE ENTIRE HOUSE!! IT WOULD TAKE AN ARMY TO CLEAN THIS PLACE! AND DON'T EVEN GET ME STARTED ON WHO CHANGES THE TOILET PAPER ROLL!!

I'm sorry. What was the question?

Male menopause is a lot more
fun than female menopause.

With female menopause you gain
weight and get hot flashes.

With male menopause you get to date
young girls and drive motorcycles.

—Rita Rudner

Unedited doctor's note:

"She has had no rigors or shaking chills, but her husband states she was very hot in bed last night."

How do you know you've reached menopause?

Your blood now goes straight
to your varicose veins.

You get food caught
in your mustache.

You buy sheets not
by their thread count,
BUT BY THEIR ABSORBENCY.

~~~~~~

You worry that you're the cause of
global warming and think Al Gore has
been following you for three days.

~~~~~~

You think, "*I know I'm still a hot babe,* but now it seems only to come in flashes."

You realize that menopause is not
a button on the DVD player.

You're certain your inner child
is playing with matches.

~~~~~~

You consider writing
a new book:
Cooking with Hot Flashes.

~~~~~~

You long for the

GOOD OLD DAYS of PMS.

Dear Tide:

I'm writing to say what an excellent product you have! I've used it since the beginning of my married life, when my Mom told me it was the best.

Now that I am older and going through menopause, I find it even better! In fact, about a month ago I spilled red wine on my new white blouse. My unfeeling and uncaring husband started to berate me about how clumsy I was and generally became a pain in the neck.

One thing led to another and I ended up with a lot of blood on my white blouse. I tried to get the stain out using a bargain detergent, but it just wouldn't come out. A quick trip to the supermarket and I had a bottle of liquid Tide with bleach alternative. To my surprise and satisfaction, all of the stains came out! In fact, the stains came out so well that some detectives who came by yesterday told me that the DNA tests were negative and my attorney said that I would no longer be considered a suspect!

I thank you, once again, for having such a great product. Well, gotta go. I have to write a letter to the Hefty bag people.

Sincerely,

A Relieved Menopausal Wife

Chapter 7

I Am Woman

Everyone's a star and deserves
the right to twinkle.

—Marilyn Monroe

The great question that has never been answered and which I have not yet been able to answer, despite my thirty years of research into the feminine soul, is "What does a woman want?"

—*Sigmund Freud*

According to a recent poll of 900,000 women, the answer to Freud's question lies somewhere between conversation and chocolate.

"How does one become a butterfly?" she asked pensively. "You must want to fly so much that you are willing to give up being a caterpillar."

—*Trina Paulus*

Nobody cares if you can't dance well. Just get up and dance. Great dancers are not great because of their technique; they are great because of their passion.

–Martha Graham

Our deepest fear is not that we are inadequate. Our deepest fear is that we are powerful beyond measure. It is our light, not our darkness, that most frightens us. We ask ourselves, Who am I to be brilliant, gorgeous, talented, fabulous? Actually, who are you not to be? You are a child of God. Your playing small does not serve the world. There is nothing enlightened about shrinking so that other people won't feel insecure around you.

We are all meant to shine, as children do. We were born to make manifest the glory of God that is within us. It's not just in some of us; it's in everyone. And as we let our own light shine, we unconsciously give other people permission to do the same. As we are liberated from our own fear, our presence automatically liberates others.

—*Marianne Williamson*

I'm not funny.

What I am is brave.

–Lucille Ball

We must have perseverance and above all confidence in ourselves. We must believe that we are gifted for something.

—*Marie Curie*

$\mathcal{I}$ am me. In all the world, there is no one else exactly like me. Everything that comes out of me is authentically mine, because I alone chose it—I own everything about me: my body, my feelings, my mouth, my voice, all my actions, whether they be to others or myself. I own my fantasies, my dreams, my hopes, my fears. I own

my triumphs and successes, all my failures and mistakes.
. . . I have the tools to survive, to be close to others, to
be productive, and to make sense and order out of the
world of people and things outside of me. I own me, and
therefore, I can engineer me. I am me, and I am okay.

—*Virginia Satir*

Imagine a woman in love with her own body.

A woman who believes her body
is enough, just as it is.

Who celebrates her body and its rhythms
and cycles as an exquisite resource.

Imagine yourself as this woman.

—Patricia Lynn Reilly